# THE FORAGE HOUSE

*poems*

TESS TAYLOR

 RED HEN PRESS | *Pasadena, CA*

Book design and layout by Christina Kharbertyan and Aly Owen

Library of Congress Cataloging-in-Publication Data

Taylor, Tess.
  [Poems. Selections]
  The forage house : poems / Tess Taylor.—First edition.
     pages cm
  ISBN 978-1-59709-270-8
  I. Title.
  PS3620.A979F67 2013
  811'.6—dc23
                              2013004264


The Los Angeles County Arts Commission, the Los Angeles Department of Cultural Affairs,
the City of Pasadena Cultural Affairs Division, Sony Pictures Entertainment, and the Dwight
Stuart Youth Fund partially support Red Hen Press. This publication was supported in part by
an award from the National Endowment for the Arts.

First Edition
Published by Red Hen Press
www.redhen.org

# ACKNOWLEDGMENTS

I am grateful for fellowships and grants from Amherst College, the American Antiquarian Society, the Berkshire Taconic Community Foundation, the Bread Loaf Writers Conference, the Headlands Center for the Arts, the International Center for Jefferson Studies, and the MacDowell Colony for support in the writing of these poems.

Thanks also to the editors of the following journals, where versions of the following poems appeared: *AGNI*, "Eighteenth Century Remains"; *American Poet*, "World's End: On the Site of Randolph Wilton"; *The Arava Review*, "Domestic Economy"; *The Believer*, "In May Whitcomb's Letters"; *Boston Review*, "Song for Sonoma"; *The Common* Online, "Official History," "Southampton County Will"; *Common-place*, "A Letter to Jefferson from Monticello"; *Guernica*, "World's End: North of San Francisco"; *Harvard Review*, "Graveyard, Monticello"; *The Hudson Review*, "Crazy Quilt"; *Literary Imagination*, "Home of the Taylors," "Museum of the Confederacy," and "Sighting"; *Memorious*, "Route 1 North, Woolwich Maine," reprinted in the anthology *Best of the Web 2008* from Dzanc Books; *Oxford American*, "Meeting Karen White, Descendant of Jefferson's Gardener Wormley"; *Painted Bride Quarterly*, "Hopkins in Winter"; *Shenandoah*, "Big Granny"; *Southwest Review*, "Reading Walden in the Air"; *Swink*, "Song for El Cerrito," reprinted in *New California Writing 2010*; *Virginia Quarterly Review*, "Virginia Pars"; *The Warwick Review*, "Altogether Elsewhere," reprinted in the *2010 Forward Book of the Poem*, London UK.

"Sighting" appeared in the chapbook *The Misremembered World*, selected by Eavan Boland, published by the Poetry Society of America, 2003.

Enormous thanks to Kate Gale and the amazing staff of Red Hen Press for care and patience; to Kevin and Brandy Barents, Elizabeth Bradfield, Camille Dungy, Rachel Richardson and David Roderick, Gabrielle Calvocoressi, Evelyn Farbman, Maureen McLane, Fred Marchant, Elizabeth Macklin, Molly Peacock and Robert Polito for friendship and thoughtful readings; to Andy Parker and Lawrence Douglas for early support; and to Jim Moran, Elizabeth Chew, Peter Hatch, Sara Bon Harper, and Cinder Stanton for help along the way.

To my family, who allowed me space to write, deep gratitude.
To Taylor and Bennett, abundant love.

*For Mary Ann Scott Clark Seelye (1921–2010)*
*& for Bennett Scott Schreiner (2011– )*

# CONTENTS

## I

## II

## III

## IV

*Yes; all these brave houses and flowery gardens*
*came from the Atlantic, Pacific, and Indian*
*oceans. One and all they were harpooned and*
*dragged up hither from the bottom of the sea.*
                                        —Herman Melville


*(I)gnorance about those who have disappeared*
*undermines the reality of the world.*
                                        —Zbigniew Herbert

I

## Big Granny

When they found Emeline, a nail
held her sack dress together

at the neck. She lived by gathering herbs
for curing leather, lived off land

her people held since they took it from the Cherokee,
quilted mountainsides in Appalachia

where they hewed walnut into rocking chairs
and sang the stony country's *blessings be*

and ballads carried in their ears from Scotland.
From my grandmother, her granddaughter,

I have one word in her dialect: *stime*.
Long-ah, half-rhyme with *steam*, its meaning: *not enough*.

As, *there's nary stime of tea nor sugar nar.*

In iron light, in the mountain graveyard
her clan's settler stones grow up with moss

thick as harmonies in shape-note tune.
In those woods, a shadowy foundation:

They took apart her house to save the boards.

# EIGHTEENTH CENTURY REMAINS

*Albemarle County*

The ridge a half mile down from Monticello.
A pit cut deeper than the plow line.
Archaeologists plot the dig by scanning

plantation land mapped *field*
for carbon, ash, traces of *human dwelling.*
We stand amid blown cypresses.

Inheritors of absences, we peer
into the five-by-five foot ledge.
Unearthed painstakingly, these shards:

two pipe stems, seeds, three greening buttons.
Centuries-old hearthstones are still charred,
as if the fire is only lately gone.

"Did they collect these buttons to adorn?" But no one knows.
"Did they trade, use them for barter?"
Silence again.

Light, each delicate pipe stem,
something someone smoked at last
against a sill-log wall that passed as home,

a place where someone else collected
wedges of cast-off British willowware.
Between vines, a tenuous cocoon.

A grassy berm that was a road.
A swaying clue
faint as relief at finding something left

of lives held here that now vanish off
like blue smoke plumes I suddenly imagine—
which are not, will not, cannot be enough.

## Mission Album 1915

May Whitcomb's children wave from their veranda.
They sling their bicycles against the jhula.
At the door, their saried ayah.

> A bullock-wallah waits with bullock cart.
> Dressed as pukka sahib, grandfather
> in the shadow of a banyan.

Along stucco walls in Ahmednagar,
shirtwaisted women pose their babies—
New New Englanders born on the Deccan.

> Men cradle guns.
> Around umbrellas, bending coolies,
> tiffins of church-picnic luncheon.

Beside the stream, mudpies;
near tamarinds, their bungalow.

> New soldiers march beyond the gates.
> The Mission quells the Empire's famines.

(They feel, even then, the shifting:
Gandhi-ji has come from Africa
"and is, it seems, determined to start something,"

writes Great-Grandfather Alden,
noting our World may not be as it's been.)

> May still makes the holiday arrangements.
> The day of Fancy Dress, her cook prepares
> stuffed chicken for American Thanksgiving.

Small Mary reads her books on Autumn,
and poses as "fallen leaf," while William
is "Red Indian Savage," feather in his cap.

     "And really," May writes, "is a perfect heathen."
     They receive hard cranberries
     from a parish off Cape Cod.

     Summon once again a pilgrim God.
Pray for succor in their wilderness.

## OFFICIAL HISTORY

You work as a journalist, pursuing legends

of other people. It is October; gold leaves fall
on your birthday.  Little mysteries

swirl with you, a *Tess*—
now hunting out a dented spoon or crest,

some half disguise by which to know yourself.
        In Boston or Brooklyn

you carry some rune, afraid of a lover,
dreading the war.

Your friends barter carbon, prepare for pandemics.
In airports you watch tarmacs

flicker through your reflection.
Leave versions of selves in the various cities.

Misplace your doppelgängers.
Little Americas, discarded paperbacks:

*O slaveholder & O bastard son.*
*O blurred stone & out-of-wedlock woman.*

## IN MAY WHITCOMB'S LETTERS

*28-11-1914, Ahmednagar, India*

Nothing is to be written on this except
the date and signature of the sender.

Sentences not required may be erased.

If anything else is added the Postcard will
be destroyed.

To avoid delay in delivery, correspondence addressed
to Prisoners of War should be written in English,
on Postcards.

*I am quite well.*
*I have been admitted to Hospital*
        *(and am going on well.)*

*I have received your (*

        *(parcel.))*

*Letter follows at first opportunity.*

## GRAVEYARD, MONTICELLO

Light silts through tulip poplars, waving.

Light gilds granite stones. Winds
hold renegade voices, fugitive

of the ravenous grave.
Roving, grieving, a confederate cry:

*Hey hullah nonny fiddle honey-child o—*
"My two hands grubbed." Jefferson's hands: his slaves.

Coffins built
in the Susquehanna foothills of the *forever mountains.*

*Appalatio Mountains.* An old west their horizon.
Now in the graveyard of these colonials,

unfinished lamentation:
Little stone, baby stone. Granite cracked with lichen.

Portal to the gone world, the old world. *Hush now.*
All your daddy's rages and drink can grow silent,

like a cruel overseer sent at last away.

## WEDDING ALBUM 1977

My parents kissing in a kitchen.
In her loop-eyed dress my mother—

enormous in her belly, I loom.
In a commune in Fort Greene

she typed and typed her dissertation.
Upstairs a woman practiced primal screams,

a wild-haired painter mourned his dying wife.
My parents had already made my life

near the mass grave
of hundreds of Revolutionary soldiers,

a cockeyed brownstone full of junkies,
somebody who stripped my parents' jalopy

down to wires and bones.
Soon they sold all they had

and drove to Madison to have me.
Had five people over for pie.

It was done then: They were married.
Weeks later in their bedroom I was born.

In piles my mother's writing
watched us from unquiet bricks and boards.

## FROM SAUSALITO IN A GRAY WIND

Fog fills the abandoned
missile site, seeps into ex-nuclear bases.
Sage & rough manzanita
clamber over shut wartime caves.

Deep in the cracking bunkers,
apocalyptic graffiti,
the plaque of a Civil War soldier
come to rest in this west-facing cold.

At this river the Miwok
gathered their willow and reeds.
The word Miwok means only *"the people."*
They burned belongings at death, but

Russian soldiers traded for baskets, so
these headlands live on in St. Petersburg.
Now fogbanks a thousand miles wide
blanket disconsolate sea bells.

The bunkers are Cold War relics.
On migrations the wind is nationless.
Hawks glide from Alaska to Mexico.
At the Farallons, the ocean deepens.

My grandmother came west and stood here.
The Blue Ridge haunted her dreams.
At this shore, she hummed mountain ballads:
                    *When first to this country a stranger I came—*

## SOUTHAMPTON COUNTY WILL 1745

I.

*I, Etheldred Taylor, of sound mind and body*
*in the presence of God almighty amen*
*do deed three things:*

        *Books Negroes Land.*
(Accumulations pass each to a son.)

I find his will, pen in hand.
Shift my books, hurt to see.

From his dim ghost I inherit
everything, nothing:

One silver teaspoon. Half a name.

II.

In another ink-smear, crazed genealogy:
Jefferson, indebted, sold his own books

to form the first national library.
He bought more.

Wrote: "I cannot live without books,"
then died in a debt greater than the nation's.

III.

In botanies, wild turkeys stalk islands,
each painted plume shimmering as
all that lay west—

              I have seen continents strewn
with theatrical objects, women's bodies
open as plunder

even in the margins of the most accurate maps.

IV.

Bestiaries, night-blooming flowers.

Model orreries. Anatomies. German philosophy.
Cabinetry, every Palladian vision—

I was taught: *He could not afford to free his slaves.*
*"Most valuable for their number ever offered at one time in the state of Virginia"*

said the newspaper his granddaughter's husband published.
FOR AUCTION: Furniture, family.

Faded ink yellow as bruises
now underscores his *"tall walls of high Rome."*

I can trace the names of his white children's descendants.
Where the enslaved went after auction

is partial—

                    not all written down.

V.

In any archive, fingering pages,
I am enthralled by gilt work, silk,

leather, the quill stroke's turn.
Feel physical want

for ink as if desiring the conquest
of tongues.  And feel my pen's weight:

Who bartered
for this parchment made with a knife?

Whose life was traded?
Luxury of blind and delicate pages.

On which spines does this volume rest?

## CRAZY QUILT

Our grandma taught her nine patch & strip piecing,
how to measure, how a fabric falls.

My sister heard her and came out a maker.
She garners fabrics, hoards a jumble pile.

She's skilled enough to half-ignore geometry,
to spread out winter evenings

and ignore us. Obbligato with the treadle's whir, she leans
into a tag-sale apron, Japanese cottons,

cambric dyed one summer in the yard.
She likes found fabric, asymmetries:

She's taught herself to work by instinct
basting light to dark, canary

to an emerald paisley:
Her expression's almost revenant

as she rips and hems and irons—
Tonight she sliced our mother's wedding sari.

Silk ribbons bloomed and I admired
her fierce concentration to resettle

even that bolt at a staggered angle,
how she hoards it, how her body stores her making,

how she destroys each blessed thing she's salvaged
to harvest it as her exploding star.

II

# WORLD'S END: ON THE SITE OF RANDOLPH WILTON

*I. Plat*

Not one *x* marks its shanties,

but I read how it was Powhatan once, a fishing camp, a dot
on John Smith's map, east of drawn-in savages dancing,
north of where his etched & tongued fires lean.

How the pit they're digging to expand
the Powhite or Pocahontas Parkway
was first salt meadow, cordgrass tributary

the English christened *World's End.*
             (Found: *A skull.* Found: *A human femur.*)
Next a Randolph port where dinghies freighted

cargo from the Chesapeake,
a hemp-tied ramp where the enslaved of Wilton
shouldered cuffed tobacco harvests.

On one plat, lacy tracery:
barns: icehouses: ferry: wharf.

Daub beam dwellings crumbled without record.

*II. Plantation*

Other bodies wait beneath the mud.

Elsewhere now, preserved, the great house,
moved for its "historic interest,"

welcomes tourists.
Regard its planks of broad New World wood.

  (—*traded what they grew in kitchen gardens*—)

Regard the portraiture, each ruff and ruche.
The era's china, framed and still.

    (*Historians speculate:*
  *an informal economy of gleaned objects*).

As if intact, each cool reconstruction.
On roads beside the gates, passing windshields

flash pewter like rare buttons in the till.

*III. Bulletin*

No one may ever find one name
of any of these unearthed dead.

Bones lie in tangled heaps while
other names emerge in wills—haphazard

property—as the hunted in police rolls,
next to notices for stolen goods,

purloined rings, watch fobs & curative elixirs.
Gull-billed terns *cre-ee* above the sedge.

> *(My negro Samuel, one crazy eye*

No paper marks these graves as family site.

> *—limps. Look for him at his mama's.)*

That violent silencing endures.
I am afraid, my friend says, of looking,

of finding nothing, a search ending in nothing.
She says, *I hallow all the disappeared.*

I feel heavy with wild namelessness.

*IV.*

O descendants, I am sorry.
Ancestors, I would undo this if I could.

*V. Map*

Just before Exit 67, purple clouds heap up.
Beyond undug graves, freeway workers

mount beams and spurs.
Atlases note the new route number. I write:

*How much I wish for will not be recorded.*

# HOME OF THE TAYLORS

*Charlottesville, VA*

The site: two acres,
rutted road up to a country chapel,

hill they granted their enslaved
"for purposes of church and school."

The Randolph-Taylors in their genteel poverty
hoarded papers. Cornelia Jefferson

ran the Ladies' Academy.
I last saw their last house in a photo:

*"Historic Homes of the Albemarle."*
Porch rockers, women in bonnets.

All specific faces blurred.
Turkey oaks, loblolly:

the land they ran for several hundred years,
lost, then bought, then lost again,

is subdivision now, a Comfort Inn.
Whatever happened here's

obscured.
The church is brick. The pastor's warm.

I went to worship. Felt
my uneasy white-girlness as I rocked.

We held hands.
Prayed. Cried *Hallelujah!*

*(May our iniquities be pardoned.)*

I wept.
Outside, fresh sunlight on the ridge.

Beneath catalpa I remembered
just one misformed family story.

After the War Bennett ran for a post in the county.
He won by the margin of "49 former servants,"

"because," he said, "they loved ole Marse Taylor."
O illuminating lie,

legend built on silence:
        I glimpse inside just as you shut your doors—

## VIRGINIA PARS

At first among certain shadows
you felt forbidden to ask whose they were.

So little to inherit: family tree, tarnished pride.
A patrician lilt to certain vowels.

Real money lost, tale crocheted
in Brockenborough doilies.

Still sad alcoholic ghosts came stalking.
Unsolved, always thinking *white* or *colored*,

they slunk by, rank as shame.
Haunted by remains

somehow you were and were not
the Confederate soldiers in your grandmother's nook.

You came
in ripped jeans from California and tasted

their seed, their curd, their underworld of 80 proof
or no proof, a difficult nut, cracked but rotten.

Known unknowns, unknown knowns
lost/not lost like the tobacco barns

on the road South, mud-daubed life
that crawled under your skin

to inhabit ensnare become partway your own.
Ghost snippets, Daddy listening

as Scotch glasses clinked, Granddaddy
killing possums with Lewis the colored man—

You felt: *This/Not this. Self/Other.*
You still wanted for them to explain

their America, their prodigal
half-remembered, always present pain.

Impossible to ask. *Don't speak of race.*
*The record's scratched. I don't recall. I never knew.*

*Anyone who'd tell you's dead.* And: *No one would tell you.*

## MARTHA JEFFERSON'S HOUSEWIFE

A woman's list: To-do and day tasks.

Red commonplace: Needle and thimble.

Light in the hand, with ivory inlay.

Her tight-lipped cursive: *Send for linen, cornmeal.*

Her *Eggs to the market. Chicken feed & Slave rations.*

*Repay money to Big George, Isaac Hemings.*

*Velvet, 4 yards: Want laces. Need Muslin.*

& one page, mid-list, her record presents,

with no explanation, a quotation from Shakespeare:

*"My poverty but not my will consents."*

# Ghost Limb

*Not, not mine. It's somebody else's wound.*
—Anna Ahkmatova

I.

Stubbly Alleghenies empty:
Bait shops, row-house valley.

A slow road fishhooks south.
In the peach grove where they camped

a sign says CORN.
Says PORN, says steakhouse, says: *sleep here now.*

Coal-poor town & crescent moon.
One neon commandment flashing:

*Souvenir!*

II.

Holiday Inns, Best Westerns, Historic Center:
Gettysburg. At 7-11, kids smoke.

I buy Cheerios. A gabled inn, electric
candles sentried in each window.

A news anchor asks me what I think of building a casino.
*Tacky*, I say. It is hot. I am sticky.

III.

Tomorrow all those years ago
somewhere among the granite

my grandfather's grandfather did not die
as his regiment was slaughtered

as they climbed the hill & splayed—

At Pickett's Charge
he survived by getting captured.

He lost & lived on. I am here now.
In these fields rough rain

still unburies unnamed bones.

IV.

Years later I winnow these shards:

How he walked home infected.
His bride was bitter. His hands shook from drink.

There was no money. His regiment was dead.
He wrote: *"we are poor now & have no servants."*

His cousin wrote:
*"Bennett is an altered person, temper unbearable selfish & inert."*

At the end of its credit, the farm mounted debt.
In the newspaper he ran:

*"smell of slave"* and *"dancing gorilla."*
*"All these free niggers should ship to Africa."*

V.

Beyond all words
silence. Afflicted. Inflicting pain.

His rage festered on.
On the field that foul sadness

rises, rears, gleams:

>*& O you stale anger,*
>*heal now—fade some—*

## MUSEUM OF THE CONFEDERACY

Inside only time
has attacked: The Confederacy's moths

have gnawed its blue wools
into tatters delicate as widows' laces.

In a reconstruction tent
Lee's tarnished bowls await no one's meal.

*To name is to claim,*
*to abandon to forget.*

Pastel dioramas display muskets at dawn.
A caption explains

how some blacks diligently followed their masters.
*(To abandon is to forget?)*

Outside the state hospital looms
smelling like sour cafeteria pizza, sweat.

The freeway overlays
the once-free-black district.

Smokers huddle in their designated spot.
Above the rosewood table

Stuart's G. Washington
*(These lamps sputtered with whale oil—),*

solemn interpretable ghost
of a "second war for independence."

*(To name is to claim:        )*
A once-belle tested her diamond with the mirror:

*he does he does not* insoluble who knows
Beyond the rococo

women's withdrawing room
the now-sick peer in at ghost heads of once-state.

The guide gives a lengthy
explanation of the fashion

for false surfaces, velvet, fake paneling.
Refers to *servants: Quelle politesse.*

Jacob Mark's roller map opens namelessly west.
Hand-sewn dolls in the nursery:

The Davis boy's toy musket.
A wild one: He made bullets then shot real people with it.

## HOPKINS IN WINTER

Grandma taught me "It is Margaret we mourn for."
I watch her sleep, catheter wobbling.

When she's awake she's partly here and partly
with Elly who Emeline took in

despite having 13 children, or the mountain doctor coming
the day she prayed God not take Nancy.

He took a chicken for his pay.
Now she's the color of old cheese above her sheets,

without that half-imperious half-charming way
she cajoles her doctors—

      just feet against blankets, in their socks.
In her apartment this October I was 8 again.

Now I'm losing both of us, how she
flirted out of Appalachia to marry a professor,

hosted dinners, quoted Frost and Austen.
Her stories garble into farming towns

she knows are gone. Memory alone roots
her world through time—

a web of ballads, spirituals, digressive eglantine
disorderly as any attic: *Hallelujah by and by.*

Listening, sifting in her wreckage,
I forage out what leafmeal worlds I can.

## ANTIQUES ROADSHOW

A fiddle plays. A coal-fired kiln.
Show & tell: A red-faced woman's

family china set (one chip), here since the 1830s.
She just loves her crazed tureen.

Junk shop musket, fired so its rifling's split
like a Damascus barrel, flintlock no one makes now,

glinting with one scar: *& kicked in what war?*
someone wants to know. German hobbyhorse,

17th century Virginia map. A then-West sprawls.
Creatures rear like beings out of Ovid.

My mother loved these, says a man, his tale wandering.
He says, *it pleases me, this curio I saved—*

for knobs for beams for what a whittler made.
Inlaid abalone, *banjo songs*

*my father's father played out on the porch,*
eyes closed, rocking. *I was small*, he says, *I swore*

*the fireflies knew the tunes.*
 Each object a clue, portent, disguise:

*I miss those songs*, he says. *I wish I knew the words.*
A man turns clay

the way his father did, knows his father's body's skill.
Pots await a glaze. In the pavilion experts finger

a child's chair, hand-hewn & much mended—
& question: *What's it worth?* & question: *Will it sell?*

# ORAL HISTORY 1963

*"Now you ladies won't you please take warning . . ."*

Year of Granddaddy Leigh in Danville.
Sign still up, dead mill
still open. He sang "Wreck of the Old '97,"

built trains in the basement.
Year my aunt M. saw colored girls at the white beach.
She wrote home "it's ok I think—I didn't tell"—

That June, for marching
in the Confederacy's last capital,
50 black men and women were beaten.

Hoses, dogs, a raw violence
deliberately unreported in the *Danville Bee*—
even blocks away it was possible

"not to know" who had been hurt by what.
    (*It's a mighty long road from Lynchburg to Danville.*)
The paper they drove to Greensboro to get

did not record the demonstrator's names. Of 50, 47
required hospitalization.
    (*Louise Pinchback, Cleveland Holt, Rev. Lawrence Campbell*—)

When these were then sentenced to fines and labor
(the law dated from Nat Turner's rebellion)
granddaddy wrote Judge Aiken

and said: "you have served to aggravate" the town's situation.
And: *"Petulant." "Inane."*
And: "I thought you should know what some people were thinking."

By Monday policemen
arrived at his office. Bench warrant.
His sentence: hard labor, double the fine.

White man, mill executive:
He made all the state papers.
Only later, standing court in his own town

he backpedaled.
Apologized.
Expressed fear for his reputation.

       Judge Aiken:
"Mr. Taylor, you should have considered your wife & children"—

## Meeting Karen White,
## Descendant of Jefferson's Gardener Wormley

My family held her family a long time, maybe five generations. We are still looking for records, which are half in the library, half in someone's attic boxes somewhere. Or destroyed. Or never existed. She wants these records. I like to garden, too, she tells me, saying how, when she found Wormley, she could see her story going on, her people there in the past—a way of imagining that grounds her. She says first it hurt to look and then it was healing. I think we are both curious to know one another, to see each other. I think so. I would not speak for her. She has come when I called her and asked. I am grateful. Our families knew each other such a long time. *Know* is not the word, someone will be upset, but it is what I want: There was togetherness, skeins of interaction we don't see. It troubles me to think that now we can't see them: the links are too painful. She told me when she found white people in her heritage she did not want to know, would stop looking, would throw away records. I told her that made sense to me, but she said she has since wanted to know them. Someone in my audience will think I am trying to make peace too easily. All I can say is that the grief of hurting is its own burden. Our grief in other people's wounds, we ward it off quickly, saying *I am not this, that is not me.* We define ourselves by *not being in that place where a torture is happening*—

She is a nurse in Fauquier County. She wears a gold cross of delicate vines. I explain I am trying to understand my roots. She says she understands: She has spent hours poring through books of records looking for families no one recorded. I tell her I could not understand my family until I understood what was not recorded. I am nervous to be there: It will not be enough, this time. Together we go to an old Randolph farm. It is beautiful in the Albemarle. Dogwood and redbud star the mountain. We drive to the gates. We knock together, hear the bell's heavy echo. Down the hill the Rivanna glints and flows on.

Wormley buried Jefferson; Jefferson sold his family. With books, with what furniture remained. Passed family among family. Human hand-me-downs. We walk past brick walls, through clipped rhododendron. We pose for a photo under a catalpa. It was here when our ancestors were. It is whorled with dark hollows. It has wide limbs, sleek pale-green buds. Someone richer than both of us owns this place now. He has collies. His son raises cattle. He says this old farm still never turns a profit. They are trying to save the brick home on the mountain from developers. The old free-black district is being torn down. Erasures are deliberate and accidental. Erasures are deliberate. We climb down together through the ice-cellar door. She says: *I feel them carrying ice here. I stand and see what they would have seen. It means so much to visit my ghosts. I can stand here and see it with them.*

She says: *I see it with them and then I leave again—*

## ROUTE 1 NORTH, WOOLWICH MAINE

Even this junk shop claims to be for sale.
       Even this junk shop comes apart. It splays

at lopsided angles where the sills
       of two half-farmhouses that formed it

separate. The porch buckles. Moldings sag.
       The whole becomes components.

For now for sale for who?
       No proper summer people will come paw.

The maples are already turning red.
       Still, of each thing here someone has thought:

*Don't throw it yet. Someone might want it.*
       *Someone might extract a value from the wreck.*

Some artist maybe.
       In real life who's got time to patch worn frames?

For rescue anyway? But if someone comes
       needing this rubble, bless him.

Bless the lobster cart beside the Dairy Queen,
       cracked enamel tubs, the sled, the screens,

the oil-smeared curtain bellying in rain.
       The cockamamie fork up on a ledge.

The forage house, its crazed assemblage:
       May someone find a window in this wind.

If the bathtub holds water, let someone
use it as a planter for geraniums.

May anyone who likes to mend, come mend.

III

# A LETTER TO JEFFERSON FROM MONTICELLO

*Westward the course of empire makes its way.*
—Bishop George Berkeley

### I

I climbed through what remains of your oak forest
& passed again our gated family graveyard

(Granddaddy's stone & Bennett Taylor's
& Cornelia J.'s & all the Marthas—)

& up the leafy slope to Monticello
& slunk into your study filled with pedestals,

translations of the Bible, Livy, Herodotus,
porcelain head of Voltaire as inkwell, plans for

an ornamental farm, Nouvelle Maison Carrée,
feeling that Rome might yet exist, forum, project

of appropriation: your America.

O hypocrite—you make me tired.
Like Whitman, you contradict yourself.

### II

Images: you, lofty, curious,
child of a mapmaker & New World aristocrat

in your one-room schoolhouse on the Randolph land grant,
learning Latin in a wilderness.

Writing that in sixteen generations
the "aboriginal" Native Americans

would be like the Britons after Caesar
& produce "their own Cicero."

Defending America's greatness
        from French snobbery with a moose.

        Nine generations later
very few of us read Cicero,

moose reclaim New England after heavy farming,
& your house is a *museum*, whose enormous gift shop

sells your profile cast in crumbly chocolate,
versions of your favorite peony

& umbrellas with your signature . . .

Here's your garden:
marrow peas asparagus

& nubbed beginnings
of the scarlet runner bean.

I still hear schoolchildren asking
why you needed slaves to grow them.

O great rhetorician, tell me: What should I say?

III

I wait
where your publics did
in the balconied front hall, your wonder cabinet.

Re-creations of buffalo-skin & beaded dress,
relics of tribal peoples
you courted Roman-style, with coins.

As tourists shuffle
off to the last buses, I hear other silence:

Behind this great hall and upstairs
a dome room and wasp-filled cuddy,
the cramped quarters of your grandchildren

who inherited your debt.


IV

Families are still stories: Now we look
for them with DNA. DNA would have
fascinated you: It is

symmetrical, almost rational,
the way you thought America's rivers would be
when you sent Lewis & Clark west

to collect & cross the continent, to gather birds & roots
& pipes & pelts & herbs & a ram's skull that hangs here,
& dialects of tribal languages, which they

subsequently lost.

>We haven't found those dialects.
>We have found DNA:
>>& tests of it suggest (though cannot fully prove)

that you had two families:
legitimate & illegitimate,
two rivers proceeding out from you—

remembered unevenly,
like names that have been saved and those
that have been lost.

>>>>Your family

made of structured absence.

>>>>>Some people in your
white family this makes furious.
Others simply wonder what a *family* is.

The word, like *freedom*, shifts
beneath us, recombinant, reforming.
Our country argues now about it.

We can't decide what it should mean.

V

Looking at the buffalo robe that is a Shawnee map

I think about asymmetry,

the ever-presence of a story we can't tell / won't see.

All stories contain opposites:

If only you look at DNA, you do not

see the whole buffalo: country: self.

Whatever frame you look through

changes what you see.

(I admire your 17ᵗʰ century micrometer, your telescope.)

We saved your hand-cast silver spectacles,

but I don't know how to see you despite

wanting to, also because of

your fractured families.

You disappear behind

your multitude of portraits.

## VI

So much (I think) of what we love about America
is hybrid like a fiddle, like rock 'n' roll, which holds

African and English rhythms meeting
near a river that in the 1800s you

called *the Cherokee Tainisee*—
                              "beautiful & navigable,"

you said. Aesthetic, practical.

A complex way of being, a difficult pose to hold.
I wondered driving down here

listening to *True Colors* & the Christian station,
how to feed body & soul. Cherries bloom

at Shadwell, near the ex-grounds of Lego

(all the lost plantations

                    where our many families lived)—


## VII

In this house museum I get special permission
to touch your bedspread, peer into your Virgil, hunt as if
for clues.

It all only looks still
but was always unfinished. You designed

porches & dumbwaiters, elaborate passages
like those beneath the Coliseum

where the Roman slaves died
in the *Panis et Circenses*. Your craft:

Keeping people hidden. I ask you:

Must beauty do this?
On what must beauty rest?


VIII

Nine generations later,

I live on a fault line.

I hike through redwood sorrel, live oak—plants you'd love to name.

Berkeley, where I grew up, is utopian, too.

Many people there build experimental gardens

& devote their lives to cultivating

the best kind of tomato: Because one has to try

to make the world a better place.

& Berkeley is segregated.

Its promise is unhealed.

>*(O & this is also inheritance from you)*—

## IX

California's road map calls it

  "geologically young and restless"—

it is literally in motion & in ten million years

will be someplace else.

Now it is coastlines, traintracks, mountains,

underfunded universities, overcrowded prisons,

factory farms, expensive cheese.

Pesticides & ocean, budget crises, artichokes.

>I learned Latin there. I re-crossed the continent.

I stand in your mote-filled sunlight in my solitary fancy.

The doors close any moment.


      Mr. Jefferson: You've also left me this.

I've never had to work in

any field except for gardens that I've planted.

I roam with a lion's share of your uneven freedom.

I pass as a dreamer, recording names.

These are beautiful & come from many languages,

reminding me how in Rome columns rear & overlap:

*Madrone: Eucalyptus: Manzanita:*

Scars themselves—unsolved or healing.

O architect of hopes and lies,

brilliant, fascinating—

ambitious foundering father I revere & hate & see myself in.

IV

## SONG FOR EL CERRITO

I used to hate its working-class bungalows, grid planning,
power lines sawing hillsides. It ashamed me
the way my parents did for not making more money.

Now it looks like a Diebenkorn.

Now I want even the bad wood siding
in our living room & my mother's aging
books on modern Indian thought.

Her tanpura in sunlight.

I want fox weed in railroad trestles,
endangered frogs in our gully.
I want a lemon tree.

On San Pablo, polyester collectibles, Mr. Bling Jewelers,

the *"All-Button Emporium: Open 10–4 only Saturday's."*
How did love lodge in these?
Marigold light

forgives even traffic islands.

December only yellows gingkoes and reddens maples.
A stream smells rich under our house.
For Christmas, my sister and I steal

persimmons from neighbors' yards.

Ten years on, I discover
how I keep falling in love here
among pickups and blackberry brambles.

Tonight it happened again:

We drove a bad car to the beach.
At dusk, a lone scrub pine—
clear, like a Japanese print. In the real sky, the moon

slid through clouds that were cinder colored.

## SONG FOR SONOMA

Dear sad ducks. Dear boats and truck.
Dear barn in the fallow field.
Dear vines in winter. Dear deer & such—

Dear power lines in a slow valley.
Dear unnamed hills on the smoggy skyline,
hills like fists or narwhals or loaves of bread.

Dear hawk & thicket, scaup pecking
a puddly traffic island; dear racetrack,
dear gimcrack & so on—

Dear tractor in lemongrass.
Dear kestrel, red-tailed hawk,
wobbly pink shed just off the road.

Dear arroyos, toyon, oyster-nacre ocean:
Now that I have your attention
I ask you to stay in the sun as you are.

Hold the bowl of the sky down with your shapes.
Hold this earth a while longer
as it swims in our vision—

## WORLD'S END: NORTH OF SAN FRANCISCO

*I. Fortress*

At the continent's end,

a river otter, lithe as compacted water,
arches through tule. A heron.

A poker-faced coyote.
Pelicans, ancient emblem of charity,

dive, spears mining water.
I know (they do not) how they were Renaissance symbols.

How here hummingbirds are Miwok gods.

*II. Ghost Town*

The Nike Missile Site: One curated missile
rises for tourists on Wednesdays.

In front, a mannequin soldier,
enclosure swallowed in foxtails.

Hikers spelunk through each bunker.
Teenagers meet up for sex.

*Battery Wallace: Battery Alexander: Battery Townsley—*
cementing the hills. *1907, '38, '63—*

bombs widened their range of destruction.
Now they seem almost Roman, these ruins.

Our conquests are going on elsewhere.
In the lagoon, hill shapes waver.

Tree forms grow obscure.
At sea, through the Golden Gate

the great *Hanjin Sea Princess*
sails west, west, to China.

*III. Compass*

As a girl I named plants here. As a pioneer
I crossed prairies by train: My life delivered me
at the mouth of the Pacific.

Ruby-throated gods fed at our bottlebrush.
I learned plant names in English.
I discovered the East

through 19th century novels and movies about New York.
That East was the past: My family came a long time ago.
After lunch I crest hills

thinking about what we drag behind us,
the inadequacy of language to place.
I examine coyote scat.

Fault-line sandstone, jarred-up plates.
I run over a seafloor
sedimented 600 million years,

between willow thickets the Spanish called *sauzalito*.
The fog is bridal, ghostful.
The foghorn sounds perfect fourths.

Plum trees from Portuguese farms
wild back into the hills.
Poison oak glints among sticky monkey.

On a serpentine outcrop, a crow.
His rasp ripens toward the ridgeline.
I stand on a crumbling fortress, making bouquets of thistle.

# READING WALDEN IN THE AIR

Somewhere above Colorado, the Rockies are spreading like ozalids, like blueprints,
the last proofs of an old-style book. Thoreau listens to the train at night,

traveling with it in mind as our stewardess arrives with pretzels.
He has measured the ice breaking, and is walking to watch skitterbugs

cross the pond's surface like aleph-bets. The Civil War has not happened yet
but brews beyond him as the seat belt light goes off.

We are free to peruse the cabin. I order tomato juice. He calls a mosquito a siren.
He ignores his Homer. Criticizes Irish laborers. Writes down the price of beans.

*Deliberate* puns on the Latin *liber*, yet he claims to read little. Still
he explains how knowledge leans westward, and also how knowledge is conquest.

Below, tracks mark the salt flats, ruts climb the Sierra. The wing floats.
By the time I reach Donner Pass, see smoke above Yosemite,

more people have visited his cottage: The woman next to me snores amiably.

## DOMESTIC ECONOMY

*—for M.A.S.*

Improbable rubble—
        phone bills pills photographs broken pens—

her scattered islands.
Preacher, mountain town,

philosopher, Maine.
Continents crossed, each faraway home.

Her kettle whined on the stove.
Briskly I'd urge her: *Throw it away.*

Instead in yard fabric rubber bands
she wove me a leapfrogging record.

Skeins of births, accidents, gravestones:
Each object earmarked a tale.

Old typefaces made her sentimental.
In her clutter democracy, wild equality bloomed.

        Eras lay open, alive—
                                quivering.

Now we only neaten her legends.
I hear my voice, keening, admonish:

  *Straighten. Be clean.*

## SIGHTING

From our bluff, the whale looked like a rock to you.
The rock looked like a whale to me.

A distance off, its slick shape broke the sea:
It heaved and dipped the way a whale might do.

We kept our watch though neither of us knew
if huge wild whale fleets really ought to be

migrating, mating, or just passing through,
or if some whales swim separately.

But when the rock looked like a whale to you,
the whale was just a rock to me.

Once it seemed to dive.  It never blew.
Again we saw the waves break and the sea

it wandered on close wordlessly
or its dark form slide out of view.

## ALTOGETHER ELSEWHERE

They multiply, these cities of the heart,
these rooms we lodge our bodies in.

Brief beds: one California night
I swam between the humpbacked coastal ranges

and woke Scotch-tinged, wet, newly dreaming
to smokestacks and sharp dawn in Queens.

Light split the branches of fresh trees.
A stage-set life implied itself from props.

Now morning— pigeon flocks, construction sites,
a Western freeway's glint, a garden filled

with verbena, sage, my childhood light—
this midsummer, too, will go so soon.

O unfinishable homes: You each feel so real so briefly.
I feel you incomplete me, incompletely.

## Bombay Archive 1975

A cavernous reading room. Two American scholars
spend days inspecting documents.

On fissured walls a Brahmin,
a Maharaja's crooked portrait.

Clerks carry up loose sheaves:
Moldering civil servants' maps, tobacco tariffs.

My not-yet mother scans the records of the Empire
to craft her history of village women.

She uses but can't trust these artifacts.

                              He catches her eye.

She's married still but soon they leave together.
They wander to the Arabian Sea.

In periwinkle night, dim kite shapes rise.
Cows paw garbage fires at dusk, and rickshaws

course between hotels with signs that read
*Inconvenience is Regretted.*

At dawn, prayers rise like minarets.
By spring my mother sings him love songs.

Dust splatters them, while expatriate and far away
the Brooklyn commune room I'll be conceived in

sleeps, unthought of yet, undreamed.
Then it's now again. We're here,

more ordinary. And, *No*, my mother says, *you haven't listened.
No, it wasn't like that really—*

# NOTES

**"In May Whitcomb's Letters"**: Those interested in prisoners' postcards as used at World War I prison camps across the world may learn more from Paul Fussell's *The Great War in Modern Memory*.

**"Southampton County Will 1745"**: On January 15, 1827 Thomas Jefferson Randolph, grandson of Thomas Jefferson and executor of Jefferson's estate, began the auction of Jefferson's possessions in the first of many attempts to settle Jefferson's debts. The sale went on for five days in cold weather. The furniture brought relatively high prices, while the 130 enslaved men and women who were for sale brought only 70 percent of their asking price. Among the bidders were Jefferson's daughters and grandchildren.

**"Virginia Pars"**: In Latin, "a part of Virginia." It is one name for the Theodore DeBry map, "Americae Pars, Nunc Virginia," which dates from 1590. After John Smith, a later cartographer was Peter Jefferson, who worked for the crown and whose map of the Virginia Colony was completed in 1751. Making the map offered him both wealth and status. It was widely considered by settlers to be the best map of Virginia for the next two generations.

**"Ghost Limb"**: Lt. Col. Bennett Taylor, great grandson of Thomas Jefferson Randolph, watched half of his regiment die at Pickett's Charge. He spent the remainder of the war imprisoned at Johnson's Island, on Lake Erie.

**"Museum of the Confederacy"**: The Museum of the Confederacy, located at the corner of Clay and Leigh Streets in Richmond, Virginia, is open to visitors Monday through Saturday 10–5 P.M.

**"Oral History 1963"**: For more information about the Civil Rights Movement in Danville, consult the Danville Virginia Civil Rights Case Files, housed in the Library of Virginia, in Richmond.

**"A Letter to Jefferson from Monticello"**: Certain lines are lifted from "A Supermarket in California," by Allen Ginsberg.

*BIOGRAPHICAL NOTE*

Tess Taylor has received writing fellowships from Amherst College, the American Antiquarian Society, the Berkshire Taconic Community Foundation, the International Center for Jefferson Studies, the Headlands Center for the Arts, and the MacDowell Colony. Her chapbook, *The Misremembered World*, was selected by Eavan Boland and published by the Poetry Society of America, and her poetry and nonfiction have appeared in *The Atlantic, Boston Review, Harvard Review, Literary Imagination, The Times Literary Supplement,* and *The New Yorker.* She currently reviews poetry for NPR's *All Things Considered* and teaches writing at the University of California, Berkeley. She lives in El Cerrito, California.